THE MAGIC OF LIFE

THE MAGIC OF LIFE

By

Brijendra Dharampuria

ISBN: 979-8-9943993-0-9 (paperback)
ISBN: 979-8-9943993-2-3 (hardcover)
ISBN: 979-8-9943993-1-6 (ebook)

For my dear parents—
the source of my strength,
my first teachers,
and my forever blessings.
You rest with the Almighty,
yet your love lives in everything I do.
Not a day goes by without remembering you.

TABLE OF CONTENTS

PREFACE

I have always believed that certain moments or incidents change completely the direction of our lives—getting married, becoming a parent, stepping into leadership, building something from nothing, and surviving what could have ended everything. I have walked through all these phases. And among them, one stands apart: I am a survivor of a tragic, near-fatal accident. That experience did not just test my strength—it transformed me. It gave me a new sense of purpose, taught me to value every breath, and pushed me to live with deeper intention.

My journey as an entrepreneur and leader shaped me just as strongly. Building businesses, leading teams, creating opportunities, and taking responsibility for people's livelihoods taught me lessons no classroom ever could. Leadership forces you to grow every day. Entrepreneurship demands courage, resilience, and the ability to rise after every fall. These experiences gave me perspectives that changed the way I see success, relationships, and life itself.

All these moments—as a son, a brother, a friend, a husband, a father, a leader, an entrepreneur, and a survivor—taught me to look at life differently. They reminded me how much potential we carry within us, even when we doubt ourselves. When you face challenges that shake your existence, you begin to live the rest of your life with greater clarity, gratitude, and strength.

As you begin this journey through the pages ahead, I hope you feel inspired, empowered, and connected. I hope this book becomes a companion during your difficult moments and a reminder during your victories. And most importantly, I hope it helps you recognize the magic that has always lived within you—waiting to be awakened and lived fully.

Welcome to *The MAGIC of Life*.

I truly hope you enjoy this journey as much as I lived it.

INTRODUCTION

This book is a reflection of my life—the mistakes that taught me, the values my parents instilled in me, and the journey that took me from one country to another.

From as early as I can remember, I carried a quiet promise inside me—a promise to create a different, better life, not just for myself but for my entire family. I grew up with humble beginnings and limited choices, yet something in me refused to accept that this was all life had to offer. I believed, even as a child, that I could rise above circumstances and shape a new destiny. That belief became the beginning of my journey.

As the years passed, life took me through highs and lows, victories and setbacks, clarity and confusion. But one thing remained constant—a deep desire to transform everything around me. And somewhere along this long road, I realized something important: What I was doing was not just an attempt to improve one life or one generation. **I was breaking patterns, rewriting futures, and changing the narrative for everyone who would come after me.**

That realization is what led me here—to writing this book.

There is a word that has always fascinated me: **magic**.

Magic is when something appears in your life unexpectedly yet perfectly—when you cannot explain how or why, but you know it is real. I witnessed this magic again and again in my own journey. Even in moments when life was falling apart or moving in unpredictable directions, something extraordinary would show up—a chance, a lesson, a person, a breakthrough. Magic continued, quietly shaping everything.

And that magic inspired me to summarize my life into a simple philosophy—one that anyone can understand, follow, and apply.

My life was full of challenges. I made mistakes, I felt confused, and for a long time, I didn't know what my true purpose was. Like many families, mine expected me to choose a safe path—a decent job and a predictable life. But that was never my calling. I wanted to do something no one in my family history had done. I wanted to create something new, bold, and meaningful. And today, when I look back, I realize that I did exactly that.

This book is not just my story. It is an invitation.

As you read each chapter, I invite you to connect every idea, every word, and every experience with your own life. Each chapter includes personal stories drawn from real moments of challenge, reflection, and growth, allowing you to see not only what I faced but also how those experiences shaped my understanding and helped me move forward.

Through these stories, my hope is that you find clarity, relatability, and the courage to reflect on your own journey. **This book is for anyone who wants to rise above their limitations, overcome their fears, and become a better version of themselves every single day.**

The philosophy in this book is simple and powerful: **MAGIC**.

It begins with allowing yourself to make **mistakes** and understanding that they are the foundation of your learning curve. Mistakes guide you, not destroy you.

Then comes your **approach**—the way you think, act, and show up in the world. With the right approach, everything becomes possible.

Next is your **goal**, because life becomes meaningful only when you understand what you truly want and commit to achieving it.

To support that goal, you must embrace **integrity**, not just as a value but as a way of living and acting. Integrity shapes your character and strengthens your journey, even when no one is watching.

And finally, the most powerful force of all—**consistency**. Because nothing in life changes unless you show up every day, even when it's hard, even when it's slow.

These five principles form *The MAGIC of Life.*

Simple. Timeless. Transformational.

CHAPTER 1
M—MISTAKES

Allowing Yourself to Make Mistakes and Build Your Learning Curve

Why This Matters

In today's world, everyone wants to be perfect on their very first try.

Kids want perfect grades.

Young adults want the perfect job.

Adults want the perfect life, the perfect career, the perfect relationships, and the perfect results.

But perfection in the first attempt is not only unrealistic—it's harmful.

It steals the beauty of learning.

It removes the space we need to grow.

It kills curiosity.

It blocks improvement.

The truth is simple:

Mistakes are not failures. Mistakes are invitations to grow.

This chapter is your reminder that you must allow yourself to make mistakes, no matter your age.

Whether you are nine or forty-five, mistakes are your most honest teachers.

A Story from My Life: "Just Do the Mistakes"

When my family moved to the USA, everything changed overnight.

New surroundings.

New faces.

New language.

New system.

New rules.

Everything felt unfamiliar—not just to us as adults but especially to my son, who was only seven years old at the time.

He was about to start his first day at a school that felt like a completely different world.

Before he stepped inside, I knelt next to him and said, "This is a new place, a new atmosphere. Enjoy it. Do what you feel is right."

He looked at me, confused, and asked the most honest question a child could ask: "How?"

How do you enjoy something when everything feels new?

How do you act when you don't know the rules?

How do you start when you don't understand the environment?

I paused for a few seconds, and then I answered, "Just do the mistakes."

That was the beginning.

He stepped into school with that mindset, and we stepped into life with the same mindset.

Why You Must Allow Yourself to Make Mistakes

Whether you're a child, a teen, or an adult, one thing remains true:

You must allow yourself to make mistakes.

Why?

Because mistakes trigger something powerful inside you:

Inner Realization: When you do something wrong, your mind quietly tells you, "I shouldn't have done that." That inner voice is your self-awareness waking up.

Emotional Understanding: Mistakes show you the truth behind your actions—your expectations, your attachments, your responsibilities, your reactions.

Beginning Self-Learning: No teacher, no school, no book can replace the lessons that come from your own experiences.

When you allow mistakes, you also allow the following:

- reflection
- understanding
- awareness

- improvement
- discipline
- mindset building

Your learning curve starts here.

What Are Mistakes, Really?

Mistakes are an inevitable part of life.

They happen to everyone—children, teenagers, adults, leaders, CEOs, even experts with decades of experience.

Mistakes don't choose people.

Mistakes don't look at age.

Mistakes don't judge your importance.

And because they are so common, most people treat them casually.

But there's a hidden beauty inside them, a gift that many people ignore:

Every mistake carries a message.

Every message offers a lesson.

Every lesson builds a learning curve.

Mistakes are not the problem.

Ignoring the lesson is.

The Trap of Ignoring (a Truth We All Experience)

None of us wants to ignore life's lessons.

Nobody wakes up and says, "I will ignore something important today."

Ignoring doesn't happen intentionally.

It happens quietly, smoothly, almost invisibly.

Many times, we tell ourselves, "I didn't ignore it on purpose."

"I didn't do it intentionally."

"I will not do this again."

Yet it still happens.

And then it happens again.

This is one of the most honest human experiences.

We don't ignore because we are careless.

We ignore because life moves fast.

We ignore because emotions overwhelm us.

We ignore because habits pull us back.

We ignore because responsibilities distract us.

Ignoring is not a decision.

Ignoring is a symptom.

A symptom of not paying enough attention.

A symptom of not slowing down.

A symptom of not giving ourselves time to reflect.

How We Learn from Ignoring

What matters is not how many times we ignored the lesson but how deeply we are willing to understand why it happened.

The moment you become aware that you ignored something important, you have already taken the first step toward wisdom.

That awareness creates responsibility.

And responsibility changes everything.

Taking Responsibility—the Cure to Ignoring

When you start feeling responsible for your actions, your mindset changes naturally.

You begin to

- think before reacting,
- observe your emotions,
- understand your patterns,
- notice your habits, and
- become honest with yourself.

Responsibility slowly reduces the "ignore symptom."

Not by force.

Not by pressure.

Not by guilt.

But through gentle awareness.

As time passes, ignoring decreases, and learning increases.

In the beginning, you may ignore a lot.

Then a little less.

Then even less.

And one day you'll realize that you no longer ignore lessons.

You catch them, understand them, and transform them.

This is how your learning curve grows.

This is how your mindset strengthens.

The Danger: Repeating the Same Mistakes

One habit we all share as humans is repeating the same mistakes.

We know something is wrong.
We know how it ended last time.
And yet we still do it again.
Why?
Because repeating mistakes is easier than changing our behavior.
It feels familiar.
It feels comfortable.
It feels automatic.
But there is a deeper truth behind this:
Repeated mistakes slowly turn into habits.

When Mistakes Become a Habit (the Real Danger Zone)

Repeating a mistake once or twice is normal.

But when the same mistake keeps returning, quietly and frequently, it begins to attach itself to your daily life.

This is where the danger zone starts.

A repeated mistake becomes connected to

- your likes and dislikes,
- your patterns,
- your reactions,
- your comfort zone,
- your emotional habits.

And that is dangerous.
Why?

Because habits run on autopilot.

They take control without asking permission.

They grow without making noise.

They build themselves without your awareness.

And suddenly, one day, you find yourself saying,

"How did this become part of me?"

"I didn't want this."

"I didn't choose this."

"I don't know why I keep doing this."

This is the silent danger of repeating mistakes.

The Turning Point: You Must Interrupt the Habit

At some point, you must stand up and tell yourself,

"I will not build this habit."

"I will not repeat this mistake again."

This is the moment when growth begins.

This is the moment when the transformation starts.

Because every time you refuse to repeat a mistake, you break one layer of the old pattern.

You stop feeding the habit.

You create space for a new version of yourself.

Mistakes will happen.

But you can decide what kind of mistakes you want to make.

Mistakes can be divided into two types:

1. **Old mistakes:** recycled, repeated, harmful, draining
2. **New mistakes:** fresh, educational, full of learning and awareness

Old mistakes keep you stuck.

New mistakes push you forward.

So tell yourself, "I am a new person every day. I have stopped repeating old mistakes. I make new mistakes—and I enjoy them because they teach me more."

This mindset is powerful.

It shifts your energy.

It gives you freedom.

It keeps you away from the danger zone of habit-building.

Embrace New Mistakes—They Lead to New Learning

When you stop repeating old mistakes, life becomes exciting again.

You begin to

- realize new lessons,
- understand new perspectives,
- improve new skills,
- strengthen your mindset, and
- grow in unexpected ways.

This is how you embrace mistakes without letting them control you.

You are not afraid of making mistakes.

You are only careful not to build habitual mistakes.

You don't stay stuck.

You stay moving.

You stay learning.
You stay growing.

How the Learning Curve Is Built

Life continues—days pass, months fly, and years move forward.

During this time, you allow mistakes.
You stay alert so as not to repeat them.
You make new mistakes.
You learn from those, too.

Slowly, without forcing anything, you begin to understand the following:

- how to behave
- how to respond
- how to control emotions
- how to communicate
- how to decide
- how to handle responsibility
- how to take better actions

This becomes your learning curve.

A learning curve is not one moment—it is a journey.
It forms your mindset.
It shapes your approach to life.

Over time, you start knowing the right mindset, the correct approach, and the balanced way to live.

This is the reward of embracing mistakes.

Mistakes Are the Source of True Learning

Always remember this:

Mistakes are not your weakness.

Mistakes are your teachers.

With the right attitude, mistakes can transform every part of your life, including the following:

- your childhood
- your friendships
- your relationships
- your career
- your business
- your habits
- your daily decisions

You can learn more from a single honest mistake than from a hundred easy successes.

Success makes you proud. Mistakes make you wise.

Both are needed, but wisdom is what carries you through life.

Why Wisdom Matters More than Ever

Look around the world today.

Powerful tools, amazing technologies, and AI devices exist everywhere.

Anyone, from anywhere in the world, can learn to use them.

Anyone can press buttons, type commands, create with AI, or operate machines.

Technology has made many things equal.

But there is one thing technology can never replace: wisdom.

Wisdom doesn't come from machines.

Wisdom doesn't come from shortcuts.

Wisdom doesn't come from copying others.

Wisdom comes from living, from trying, from failing, from making mistakes, and from learning every time you rise again.

The people who will lead the future are not those who know the most tools—they are the ones who understand themselves.

In a world where everyone has the same tools, wisdom becomes your unique trait—your special advantage.

A Simple Practice: Daily Self-Scanning

Here is a small exercise.

Do it every day—morning, evening, or night.

Just give yourself five minutes.

Sit quietly.

Close your eyes.

Talk to yourself.

Scan your day.

Ask one simple question:

"What did I learn today?"

Maybe you learned not to react quickly.

Maybe you learned to listen more.

Maybe you learned patience.

Maybe you learned something about people.

Maybe you learned something about yourself.

Every answer becomes one step on your learning curve.

Final Message: The Power of Mistakes

Mistakes are not failures; they are invitations to grow. They awaken awareness, sharpen thinking, and open the doorway to self-understanding. Through mistakes, we experience inner realization, emotional understanding, and self-learning. Over time, this process strengthens our character and evolves our approach to life.

The real danger appears when mistakes are repeated without reflection. When lessons are ignored, mistakes slowly turn into habits that hold us back. Mistakes themselves are never the problem—ignoring what they are trying to teach us is.

Every mistake carries a message, every message reveals a lesson, and every lesson builds our learning curve. This is how growth becomes continuous and meaningful. Success may make us proud, but mistakes make us wise—and it is wisdom that carries us through life.

Life is a long, beautiful journey, and throughout that journey, your greatest teacher is always you. You guide yourself, correct yourself, and build yourself. Mistakes are not the ending; they are the beginning.

CHAPTER 2
A—APPROACH

Learning to Develop and
Create the Right Approach

Mistakes Begin the Learning Curve,
but Approach Shapes the Climb

Mistakes are the beginning of your learning curve. They push you to think, reflect, and understand yourself better.

But what decides whether you rise from those mistakes or stay stuck in them is your approach.

Mistakes create awareness.

Approach creates direction.

After learning from mistakes, the next step is building the right mindset—one that is open, curious, and ready to improve.

Only then can you understand the true value of a correct approach.

A closed approach looks at mistakes as signs of failure.

A strong approach looks at mistakes as messages: "This is where I can grow."

Your approach is what turns experiences into lessons and lessons into progress.

It is what shifts fear into confidence, confusion into clarity, and hesitation into action.

Talent may help you start, but **an approach enables you continue, grow, and achieve**

This is why approach always matters more than talent—

because talent can fade,

but a correct approach keeps evolving with every step you take.

Why Approach Shapes Your Life

Every person has dreams, but not everyone reaches them.

What creates the difference?

Not luck.

Not talent.

Not opportunity.

It is the approach a person carries toward life.

Your approach is the way you think, act, react, plan, and solve problems.

It is the engine behind every decision.

It decides how you use your time, how you learn from mistakes, and how you move forward when things become difficult.

Approach is the doorway through which your potential becomes reality.

The Power of a Priority-Aligned Approach

When your priorities and approach are aligned, life becomes smoother.

Your mistakes turn into lessons.

Your decisions become easier.

Your direction becomes clearer.

Your energy gets focused.

Your progress becomes visible.

The formula is simple but powerful:

- Set the right priorities.
- Build an approach that matches them.
- Apply consistency.
- Adjust as you grow.

This alignment creates steady, meaningful progress—not through luck but through clarity and intention.

A correct approach begins with clarity of priorities.

Your priorities determine what you focus on, how you invest your energy, and how you direct your thoughts.

If your priority is learning, you develop a disciplined approach.

If your priority is earning, your approach becomes driven by that.

If your priority is personal growth, your approach becomes thoughtful and intentional.

This is the true strength of having priorities.

Your approach follows your priorities the way a river follows its path.

Design the path wisely, and your life flows in the right direction.

Time Is Equal; Approach Is Not

Everyone has the same twenty-four hours.

Yet some people seem to accomplish so much, while others struggle to get through simple tasks.

It isn't the number of hours that matters—it's the approach behind those hours.

A person with a clear approach

- knows what must be done,
- focuses on what matters,
- avoids unnecessary distractions, and
- uses time with purpose.

When your approach is shaped by priorities and supported by the learning curve, you naturally become more efficient.

And with time, that efficiency becomes a part of who you are.

That is how ordinary days turn into extraordinary progress.

A Real Story: When Everything Changed

Let me take you back to the early days of COVID-19.

One announcement changed everything: offices closed, life paused, and uncertainty grew everywhere.

I still remember telling my team, "Take your laptops and go home. We'll figure out how to continue."

Inside, I wondered,

How will we adapt?

How will we support each other?

How will we manage work from home?

It was clear that the approach that worked before could no longer support us.

We needed a new direction—quickly and wisely.

This moment taught me the importance of reshaping the approach when life changes unexpectedly.

Rebuilding My Approach During the Toughest Days

During those months of uncertainty, I restructured almost everything: communication methods, work processes, delivery systems, leadership style, team training, expectations, priorities.

I worked long hours—not out of pressure but out of necessity and responsibility.

The situation outside was difficult, but redefining my approach allowed our entire team to stay strong.

This experience became one of the most meaningful phases of my life because it reminded me of this:

When the environment changes, your approach must evolve.

That's how you survive—and then grow.

Efficiency + Accuracy = a New Version of You

As you align your approach with your priorities, something remarkable begins to unfold.

You start working faster without rushing.

Your actions become sharp and purposeful.

Your decisions feel clearer and more confident.

You gain the energy to take on more without feeling overwhelmed.

You begin to trust yourself in a new way.

Efficiency helps you use every minute wisely.

Accuracy ensures every effort counts.

When these two combine under the guidance of the right approach, you unlock a level of performance that sets you apart from others.

But here is the truth most people ignore:

Reaching this level requires real involvement—not just from the mind but from the deepest part of you.

A correct approach supported by efficiency and accuracy cannot be built casually.

It needs awareness, discipline, consistency, and a genuine desire to grow.

You must stay connected to your priorities because the moment your priorities slip,

your approach weakens, your efficiency drops, and your accuracy becomes unstable.

This entire level of living grows slowly through daily commitment.

You maintain it by being present, observant, and honest with yourself.

It takes learning, adjusting, correcting, and real self-involvement.

Every day you stay aligned, every day you give your best attention, and every day you act with intention, your approach becomes stronger and more natural.

This is how you become the version of yourself that

- thinks clearly,
- acts wisely,
- works efficiently,
- produces accurate results, and
- stays centered even when life gets difficult.

Efficiency and accuracy are not just achievements— they are the reflection of deep involvement, strong priorities, and a correct approach practiced day after day.

Final Message: Build Your Approach

You don't need a perfect background, perfect conditions, or perfect talent to improve your life.

What you truly need is the willingness to shape your approach every single day.

A correct approach is not built in one moment—it is built through daily involvement, small improvements, honest reflection, and clear priorities.

Here's how you start creating the life you want:

1. Begin with Awareness. Every improvement starts with noticing what you're doing, why you're doing it, and what needs to be corrected.

Spend a few minutes each day quietly asking yourself,

"Is my approach today matching the priorities I've set for my life?"

This simple check brings focus and resets your direction.

2. Practice Daily Observation. Take one person every day— anyone: a friend, a colleague, a teacher, a family member, a stranger, even a child.

Observe how they behave, how they work, how they react, how they manage time, or how they handle pressure.

You will be surprised at how much life teaches you when you pay attention.

Observation gives you insight.

Insight strengthens your approach.

Sometimes you learn what to do.

Sometimes you learn what not to do.

Both help you grow.

3. Accept Comments and Criticism with Maturity. Not every comment is meant to hurt you.

Some comments—even sharp ones—hold truth.

When someone gives feedback, pause before reacting.

Ask yourself, "Is there something useful here for me?"

If yes → take it and adjust your approach.

If no → stay calm and move forward.

The ability to receive words without feeling attacked is a major step toward personal strength.

Start today.

Your future is created by the approach you choose now.

CHAPTER 3
G—GOAL

Understanding the True
Meaning of Setting Goals

Entering the Third Pillar of MAGIC

Now that we have traveled through the first two pillars of the MAGIC of Life—understanding mistakes and developing the right approach—it is time to step into the next powerful chapter: Goal.

Your mistakes shaped your foundation.

Your approach shaped your direction.

Now your goals will shape your destination.

But before we discuss how to set goals, we must ask,

Do we truly understand what a goal is?

Most people talk about goals, plan goals, and even set goals, but very few understand the true essence of what a goal actually means.

This chapter is not just about setting goals—it is about discovering the deeper meaning behind them.

Let's begin this journey of understanding.

What Exactly Are Goals?

A goal is not just a task or a checklist item.

It is not simply a wish or a dream.

A goal is a cluster of meaningful milestones—achievements, progress, life events, habits, or improvements—that matter to you, your family, your friends, and your well-wishers.

A goal is something that holds emotional value and personal/professional importance.

What's interesting is that we all love talking about goals. We enjoy discussing them, writing them down, and planning them. But very few ever pause to understand the true essence of why we set them.

Before you set another goal, you must understand what gives a goal its power.

Understanding the True Meaning of Goals

The essence of setting a goal is always connected to one powerful element: purpose.

Without purpose, a goal is just a sentence on paper.

With purpose, a goal becomes a mission.

Purpose gives meaning.

Purpose brings clarity.

Purpose fuels the journey.

Just as mistakes become meaningful when a mindset is

attached, an approach becomes effective when a priority is attached.

Similarly, a goal becomes powerful when it is given purpose.

Purpose is the invisible force that ties your goals to your life journey—from your mistakes to your growth, from your priorities to your values.

Without purpose, goals collapse.

With purpose, goals flourish.

Learning the Purpose Behind the Goal

Purpose is not something you write just to complete an exercise.

It is much deeper than that.

Purpose answers the question, "Why do I want this goal?"

A strong purpose:

- Gives you clarity
- Strengthens your commitment
- Makes your actions meaningful
- Helps you stay focused
- Supports you during difficult days

A goal without purpose constantly needs external motivation.

A goal with purpose creates internal motivation that never stops.

Purpose is the reason that keeps you moving when progress feels slow.

Purpose is the anchor that keeps you steady when life gets tough.

When you know why, you will find your how.

The Power of Self-Motivation

Self-motivation is the engine of success.

Most people depend on external motivation—a video, a speech, a book, or a friend's encouragement.

These things help, but they fade quickly.

Real achievement comes from self-generated motivation—the kind that grows from within you, from your purpose, your belief, and your commitment.

Every goal you achieve builds a new layer of confidence inside you.

Each milestone you hit strengthens your belief in your abilities.

This is the biggest gift of goal-setting: It teaches you how to self-motivate for life.

Self-motivation becomes your internal power source.

It carries you through failures, challenges, and difficult phases.

It helps you rise, no matter how many times you fall.

Disconnecting Goals from Roles

Most people attach their goals to their roles:

- job titles

- responsibilities
- life positions
- social status
- relationship roles

But roles change.

Titles change.

Situations change.

If your goals depend on your role, they will keep changing too.

That's why it is important to remember this:

Your goal must be disconnected from your role.

Your goals should reflect the following:

- your inner calling
- your values
- your identity
- your long-term vision

Not your current role in life.

When goals rise from within you rather than from your temporary role, they become pure, stable, and future-proof.

Adapting: The Bridge Between Purpose and Progress

Once your mindset is aligned, your approach is clear, your priorities are defined, and your purpose is strong, one element determines whether you move forward or remain stuck: **adaptation**.

Adaptation is not a choice reserved for comfort.

It is a necessity revealed during life's hardest moments.

To truly understand this, I must share a defining chapter of my life.

It was the year 2017.

A tragic car accident changed everything in a matter of seconds.

I lost four members of my family, including my parents.

I was the only one who survived.

There are moments that divide life into *before* and *after*.

That moment was mine.

I still remember those seconds—seconds where I knew what I had lost, seconds where I believed my life was ending too, seconds where everything familiar disappeared.

Surviving was not the victory people imagined.

The real challenge began after.

Every passing day carried the weight of grief.

Silence became louder than noise.

Memories felt heavier than reality.

And the question that stayed with me was not *"Why did this happen?"* but *"How do I live from here?"*

I stood at a crossroads.

One path was to remain trapped in loss.

The other was to adapt.

Adaptation did not mean forgetting.

It did not mean moving on easily.

It meant learning how to live again—breath by breath, step by step—with a completely different understanding of life.

I had to rebuild

- my inner strength,
- my emotional balance,
- my purpose,
- my reason to move forward.

The life I was meant to live ended that day.
The life I chose to live began after that.
So I adapted.
I restarted from where everything broke.
Not because it was easy—but because it was necessary.
And this is why adaptation matters.

Because somewhere, right now

- someone is struggling more than they ever imagined;
- someone is facing a deeper fall;
- someone feels lost at the edge of hope.

If you are reading this, remember: If rebuilding was possible for me from that moment, it is possible for you too.
Adaptation does not erase pain.
But it transforms pain into progress.

It keeps you moving.

It realigns your purpose.

It protects your goals.

And it helps you rise—not as who you were, but as who you are becoming.

Adaptation is not just survival.

It is the bridge between purpose and progress.

Valuing Life and Enjoying the Journey

After such a phase in my life, my understanding of life changed forever.

When you stand that close to loss, you realize something very clearly—**nothing is guaranteed, and everything can be gone in seconds.**

From that moment, I stopped measuring life only by outcomes.

I started valuing the **journey itself**.

Goals no longer felt like pressure.

They became a **direction**.

They became a **smooth ride** instead of a burden.

They became a way to feel alive, not a race to finish first.

That is when I truly understood this truth:

Goals are not meant to stress life.

They are meant to make life meaningful.

Enjoy the phase of planning your goals.

Enjoy discovering yourself through them.

Enjoy the process of becoming better—not perfect.

Enjoy the small wins that quietly build confidence.

Enjoy the big wins that remind you of your strength.

Because life does not become beautiful when you arrive—
life becomes beautiful while you are moving.

Build Your Surroundings Wisely

When you truly begin to value life, you also begin to value who you share it with.

Enjoying the journey is never a solo experience.

It is deeply connected to the people around you—

The people you sit with.

The people you eat with.

The people you cry with.

The people you laugh with.

The people who listen to you.

The people who support you.

These people shape the energy of your life.

Healthy surroundings make the journey joyful.

Toxic surroundings make the journey heavy.

When you surround yourself with positive, loving, strong, supportive people, you enjoy life more deeply.

You stay motivated.

You stay consistent with your goals.

You feel emotionally safe.

You grow faster.

You inspire others through your journey.

Your surroundings don't just influence your life—they become part of your success.

So choose your surroundings intentionally.

Build a circle where love, growth, and inspiration flow freely.

Because when you grow, your surroundings grow.

And when they grow, they lift you even higher.

This is how you create a life full of joy, motivation, and meaningful progress.

Final Message: The Essence of Goals

As we complete this chapter, remember that goals are not just targets—they are the direction of your life energy. Goals help you rise after your mistakes, walk with purpose, and shape the life you dream of.

A goal without purpose is empty.

A purpose without action is incomplete.

And an action without adaptation is unstable.

Your goals become powerful when you understand the following:

- Where you came from (your mistakes)
- Who you are becoming (your mindset)
- How you walk the path (your approach)
- What matters most (your priorities)
- Why do you want it (your purpose)
- How you rise again (your adaptation)
- Who you bring along (your surroundings)

And at the center of everything is this quiet reminder: Love yourself. Respect yourself. Trust yourself.

Because you are the one walking the journey.

You are the one facing the storms.

You are the one building your future.

Your goals are not promises to the world—they are promises to your future self.

Keep them.

Protect them.

Live them.

This is the MAGIC of Life.

CHAPTER 4
I—INTEGRITY

Understanding How Integrity Builds Character, Success, and Inner Strength

Integrity: The Invisible Foundation

We often admire discipline, ambition, intelligence, talent, and resilience.

Yet there is one quality that quietly determines the direction, strength, and longevity of all successes: integrity.

Integrity is not a decoration you wear in public; it is the quality of your actions when no one is watching. It is the silent, private decision-making system that drives your behavior in moments where shortcuts look sweeter than honesty, where the world permits you to cheat because "everyone else does it," where the situation is unfair, biased, or painfully inconvenient.

In your MAGIC of Life journey, you must anchor your life with unshakable integrity.

Without it, everything you build will eventually collapse or will not be respected.

With it, everything you build stands taller with time.

The Real Test Happens in the Dark

It is easy to act good in public.

It is easy to look respectful on social media.

It is easy to behave wisely when the world is watching.

But how do you act when you are alone?

How do you act when things are unfair?

How do you behave when the circumstances tempt you to bend your values because the reward is huge?

How do you react when others behave poorly, when the environment favors the wrong people, when shortcuts seem faster, and when honesty feels like a disadvantage?

Integrity is revealed not in your comfort but in your chaos.

It is shown in how you choose to respond to challenges that test your values, identity, and self-control. These moments decide the type of person you become, regardless of what degrees you hold or how much money you earn.

The world measures your success.

But you measure your own integrity.

And if you fail in your own eyes, nothing else can fill that emptiness.

Integrity Shapes Your Long-Term Self

You can become highly educated, wealthy, loved, or famous. But if you lose integrity, you lose the only thing that holds all your achievements together: yourself.

Integrity becomes the mirror you cannot escape.

It is the voice that speaks to you at night.

It is the standard you judge yourself by.

People can forget your accomplishments.

People can misunderstand your intentions.

People may never see the full story of your life.

But you know the truth about your choices.

And that truth stays with you forever.

In the long run, it's not your connections, background, or talent that shape your destiny—it's your inner moral architecture.

Integrity creates a legacy that continues into the next generations because your children, your family, and your people inherit not just your wealth but your values.

Why Integrity Matters Even More When You Grow

As you grow—personally, professionally, financially—life gives you more freedom, more flexibility, and more power to shape your world. Ironically, this is also when you become most vulnerable.

When you start achieving, you feel unstoppable.

When you start gaining influence, you feel important.

When you receive respect, you feel validated.

When money flows, you feel in control.

And here lies the danger.

The higher you climb, the stronger the temptation to loosen your principles.

You begin thinking, "I have earned this. I can do what I want."

And slowly, without realizing, people collapse under their own success.

Success without integrity becomes a trap.

It makes you feel invincible until the first wrong step exposes the weaknesses inside your foundation.

This is why integrity must be planted early—in your school days, early jobs, college years, and early business experiences. When you build integrity early, you do not have to "learn" it later when your stakes are much higher.

My Personal Story: A Real Test in the Western World

The story I'm about to share shaped my soul and forever strengthened my belief in integrity.

I am a first-generation, real-from-scratch builder of my destiny.

Every lesson came from pain.

Every step came from trial and error.

Every achievement came from following MAGIC.

During one of the most defining phases of my journey, I traveled alone on a long business tour across the USA.

Weeks of moving from one city to another.

Meeting people from every background.

Staying alone in hotels.

No family watching.

No society judging.

No colleague noticed my behavior.

When you are alone in a foreign land, that's when the real you comes out.

You get opportunities—not always good ones.

You face temptations—not always harmless.

You experience loneliness—not always easy.

You feel the freedom—not it is not always safe.

One wrong move could have destroyed everything I built.

One small compromise could have damaged my name, my future, my peace.

One bad habit could have changed the direction of my life forever.

But every time temptation knocked on the door, I reminded myself:

Remember your roots.

Remember your parents' struggles.

They fought battles you didn't see so you could stand where you are today.

Remember your sacrifices.

You did not come this far to throw everything away for a shortcut.

Remember the tough phases you survived.

You are stronger than your weakest temptation.

Remember your family who loves you unconditionally.

They trust you—do not break that trust.

Remember that you are the only one watching yourself every day.

If you lose respect for yourself, nothing outside can replace it.

Remember that life is long.

One wrong move can affect decades—but one right move can elevate future generations.

Your roots are your anchor.

When you remember where you come from, you always know who you should be.

And just like that, I passed the toughest examination of my life—not because I was perfect but because I was rooted.

Integrity saved me.

Integrity shaped me.

Integrity protected the destiny I was building.

Once you go through such experiences, you don't just "believe" in integrity—you become a product of it.

Integrity Builds Inner Strength and Self-Discipline

When you protect your integrity, you build something far greater than a reputation—you build your inner mastery.

Integrity teaches you

- self-discipline when temptations appear;
- resilience when the environment is unfair;
- courage to stand alone if needed;
- patience to choose long-term wins over short-term relief;
- respect for yourself and your journey;
- consistency, even when no one is watching.

Integrity becomes your silent superpower—the kind of strength that doesn't need to shout, show off, or prove anything.

This inner strength is what high achievers rely on when life tests them.

It is what keeps champions grounded when success tries to blind them.

It is what separates leaders from followers, visionaries from imitators, and achievers from pretenders.

Protect Your Integrity at All Costs

No matter how difficult life becomes or how tempting the shortcuts are, never allow anyone to shake your integrity.

Not friends.

Not colleagues.

Not society.

Not money.

Not opportunities.

Not fame.

Not frustration.

Not pressure.

Your integrity is your compass.

If you lose it, you will lose your direction.

Whenever life forces you into tough decisions, always ask yourself,

"If my parents and my future children were watching me right now, would I be proud?"

If the answer is no, don't do it.

If the answer is yes, keep going, even if it's hard.

Integrity might slow you down temporarily, but it guarantees you will never collapse permanently.

The Price of Losing Integrity

You lose trust.

You lose respect.

You lose credibility.

You lose opportunities.

You lose relationships.

You lose peace.

You lose yourself.

Even one moment of compromise can damage years of hard work.

No matter how talented or smart you are, without integrity, your success becomes temporary. People may admire your wins, but they will never trust your character.

And trust—not money, not fame, not talent—is the real long-term currency of life.

Final Message: Scan Your Life Every Year

Just as we update our phones, cars, or business systems, we must update our inner system too.

Every year on your birthday—or any day you choose— take time to evaluate yourself honestly.

Did I stay true to my values this year?

Did I act out of honesty even when life was hard?

Did I protect my integrity when no one was watching?

Did I become better than I was last year?

What did I learn from my mistakes?

Which habits need to be removed?

What part of my character needs strengthening?

This annual self-scan keeps your integrity sharp, your direction clear, and your identity rooted.

Growth is not just about achievements; growth is about becoming a better human every year.

Be the person you can respect.

At the end of the day, life brings you many roles—parent, partner, entrepreneur, creator, leader, dreamer. But before all these roles, you must first become a person you genuinely respect.

Integrity is the commitment you make to yourself.

"I will not betray who I am, even if the world does."

This commitment becomes your silent guide through all the highs and lows of life. It becomes the seed from which your courage, confidence, peace, and long-term success grow.

You do not need to be perfect.

You do not need to be flawless.

You only need to be honest with your own soul, consistent with your values, and strong enough to act on them when the world tests you.

Because in the end…

Integrity is not what you show to the world.

Integrity is who you choose to be when no one is watching.

CHAPTER 5
C—CONSISTENCY
Adopting and Acting on the Principle of Consistency

The Quiet Force Behind Every Great Life

This final chapter is reserved for consistency because it is the heartbeat of everything you've learned. Mistakes teach you, approach guides you, goals drive you, and integrity grounds you, but without living them day after day, they lose their purpose. Consistency keeps them alive.

Consistency is not loud.

It is not dramatic.

It does not seek attention.

But it builds everything.

Consistency is the bridge between knowing and becoming, between wishing and achieving. It is the daily discipline, the routine, the decision you make every morning when the world is still quiet.

"I am still showing up."

This is why consistency matters.

Because without it, even the strongest intention remains only a thought.

Why Consistency Is the Most Important Principle

Dreams demand commitment.

Success demands patience.

And all these demand consistency.

Your life journey begins with excitement—love, curiosity, hope. But reaching your destination requires a different energy: endurance. There will be times of rest, moments of pause, and seasons where life feels heavy. But consistency ensures that even on those days, you do not abandon your path.

We all want the feeling of achievement.

We all want to experience success.

But the truth is simple and universal: **Consistency is the *key* that unlocks the door to your destination.**

Consistency is a mindset before it is a behavior.

It begins when you do the following:

- Allow yourself to make **mistakes**.
- Learn from those mistakes instead of fearing them.
- Accept challenges instead of avoiding them.
- Build a strong **approach** instead of a weak excuse.
- Define your purpose clearly until it becomes unshakable.

- Set **goals** that stretch you.
- Surpass those goals intentionally.
- Hold **integrity** as your compass.

When you do these things, **Consistency** stops being effort—it becomes your identity.

How to Become Consistent

Consistency is the connection between your destination and the effort required to reach it. It is built through perseverance, continuous effort, and day-to-day follow-ups—the quiet work that moves life forward. And to maintain this consistency, you must stay deeply connected to where you are heading.

When you clearly understand your destination, every phase of the journey becomes manageable. Even when you feel low, tired, or discouraged, that connection reminds you why you started. You can speak to yourself, realign your focus, and reignite the same fire within you.

Consistency doesn't mean you will never fall—it means you always return.

It means you recharge, reset, and begin again with the same commitment.

That connection to your destination becomes your inner voice, your strength, and your reminder that no matter how tough the phase is, you are capable of getting back up and moving forward.

Be consistent in every process, every phase, every emotion, and every challenge of life.

To adopt it, you must strengthen your relationship with yourself. Believe in yourself more than ever. Let that belief guide your actions.

Action Creates Consistency and Becomes Success
You do not "become" consistent.
You act consistently.
It starts small—by showing up every day, no matter what.
Show up on your good days.
Show up on your tired days.
Show up on the days you doubt yourself.
Show up even when nothing seems to be happening.
Your action sends a message to your mind:
"I am someone who follows through."
Every time you show up, you build a new version of yourself—stronger, clearer, focused.
Consistency is not built into big decisions.
It is built on the tiny choices repeated over time.

The Routine of Success
Here is the truth nobody talks about:
Success is boring.
Not because success is uninteresting, but because the process that creates success is repetitive. It might feel like you're doing the same thing again and again, but this repetition is what forms mastery.
When boredom comes, remember: This is not a problem. This is a signal that you are building something powerful.
Learn to love this boredom.

This boredom is the early stage of transformation.

This boredom is preparing the MAGIC of Life.

Tell yourself, "This is the new me—the me who is consistent even when it feels boring."

That version of you becomes unstoppable.

Consistency Is a Dialogue with Your Future Self

Every consistent action you take is a message to your future self.

A promise.

A gift.

When you act consistently today, you make tomorrow easier.

When you act consistently tomorrow, the next week becomes stronger.

When the next week is strong, the next month becomes transformative.

Your future self is waiting for you.

And consistency is how you walk toward it every single day.

The Compound Effect of Consistency

Consistency does not give instant results.

It gives compounded results.

Just as water does not boil at 95°C, success does not appear at 95 percent effort.

It comes when you keep going, keep showing up, keep repeating, until that last 5 percent suddenly creates a breakthrough.

People will call it luck.

But you will know the truth.

That breakthrough was built by the thousands of small, invisible moments when you chose consistency over comfort.

That is your magic.

You created it.

And the best part?

Consistency is 100 percent in your control.

Every day you show up, you rewrite your story.

Every day you commit, you move closer to your destination.

Every day you repeat, you build your identity.

And eventually, you become the person you always wanted to be.

This is the principle you must adopt.

This is the principle you must act upon.

This is the principle that transforms your life.

Be consistent.

Be unstoppable.

Be you—in your best, strongest version.

A Personal Reflection—Consistency Changed My Destiny

I clearly remember a phase of my life when I was wholly lost.

I didn't know where I was going or what I would become.

Coming from a very ordinary family with simple expectations, I was nowhere close to the life I live today.

Almost everyone around me had quietly lost hope that I would do anything meaningful.

During that period of uncertainty, I did what many people do when they feel powerless I visited someone who practiced palmistry and horoscope reading, hoping for direction.

He studied my palm, my horoscope, asked me a few questions, and then sat in silence for a while.

What he said next stayed with me forever.

He told me that whatever I was at that moment, whatever I was doing, and whatever I had—life would become even more difficult ahead.

Then he added one powerful line: "Only consistent hard work can change your destiny."

I returned home disturbed, but something within me shifted that day.

I had always believed that something external would change my destiny—luck, opportunity, support, or a sudden breakthrough.

But that day, I understood a more profound truth: my destiny was in my own control.

From that moment on, I began doing everything with greater perseverance, sharper awareness, and disciplined effort.

I learned to combine hard work with smart thinking.

Most importantly, I learned the power of showing up every single day.

That is when consistency entered my life—not as a concept, but as a way of living.

And today, I can say this with complete certainty: Consistency is always in your control.

When you commit to it, you don't just change your habits—you change your direction, your mindset, and eventually, your destiny.

CONCLUSION
THE PROMISE OF BECOMING

To every reader turning the last page of this book—whether you are stepping into your double digits or entering your twenties, thirties, or forties—this conclusion is written for you.

This book is not just a guide.

It is a mirror.

A compass.

A reminder.

A beginning.

It exists to show you that life is not about being perfect—it's about becoming.

Becoming wiser.

Becoming stronger.

Becoming more aware of what shapes you and what you choose to shape in return.

Your journey begins with **mistakes**.

You will allow them. You must make them. Because mistakes don't destroy you—they prepare you. They open your eyes, stretch your understanding, and awaken the mindset needed to rise. Mistakes are not the end of the path; they are the introduction to it. From your mistakes comes your mindset—the way you think, react, believe, and choose. When your mindset grows, everything in your life rises with it.

Then comes your **approach**—the energy you bring into the world. Approach is your behavior, your tone, your discipline, your attitude. But an approach without priorities is like a map without a destination.

That's why they must walk together.

Approach defines direction; priorities define speed.

With the right approach and the right priorities, life becomes clearer, simpler, and more meaningful.

As you grow, you will begin shaping your goals, not just dreams in your mind but real, meaningful targets that guide your life forward. But remember: **Goals need purpose.**

Purpose is what gives your goals a heartbeat. Purpose anchors you when you feel lost and pushes you when you feel tired.

You will keep evolving through adaptation because life will shift—again and again. Plans will change. People will change. You will change, but adaptation keeps you flexible and alive.

Build your surroundings. The people and influences around you will shape who you become more than you realize.

Choose wisely.

Choose intentionally.

Choose people who lift your spirit, add to your wisdom, and strengthen your character.

And through all your growth, challenges, victories, and seasons, one thing must remain close to your heart: wisdom.

Wisdom is not loud. Wisdom is not proud.

Wisdom is the quiet, honest voice that guides you back to yourself.

When you allow mistakes, strengthen your mindset, align your approach with your priorities, build purposeful goals, choose your surroundings, and walk with wisdom, something beautiful happens.

You begin to live with **integrity**—the truth that holds your character together.

Integrity shapes your trust, your relationships, your peace, and your legacy.

And finally, the quiet force that transforms everything: **consistency**.

Small actions, repeated daily, become the foundation of lifelong change.

So as you move through each stage of life, remember this:

You are not expected to be perfect.

You are expected to become.

Here is your final promise—spoken not to the world but to yourself:

I will allow mistakes but never repeat them.

I will choose a mindset that lifts me.

I will refine my approach and protect my priorities.

I will create goals with purpose.

I will adapt with grace and value life.

I will build surroundings that shape my success.

I will protect my integrity when no one is watching.

I will walk every day with wisdom and consistency.

Your life is not just something to live—it is something to shape, to elevate, and to become.

Welcome to the MAGIC of Life.

This is your promise. This is your journey.

This is your becoming.

THE LIVING PAGES

These pages are intentionally left spacious.

Write freely, underline words, draw lines, or simply note one powerful sentence.

Return to these pages whenever life teaches you something new.

Mistakes and Awareness

Please write down your answers.

My habit (my real danger zone):

____

____

My trap of ignoring:

____

____

My responsibilities (my cure to ignoring):

____

____

What these mistakes have taught me (my learning curve):

____

____

One sentence I must remember: "If I repeat this mistake, I know exactly why."
Return to this page often. Awareness is the first win.

Approach and Priorities

Please write down your answers.

My old approach that no longer serves me

____

____

My new approach going forward:

____

____

My top three priorities in this phase of life:

____

____

What I will say no to more often:

____

____

Daily reminder: "Not everything deserves my energy."

Goal with Clear Purpose

Please write down your answers.

My primary goal with a clear purpose:

____

____

Why this goal truly matters to me:

____

____

Who are my surroundings:

____

____

Who I am becoming while pursuing it:

____

____

One commitment to myself: "Even on hard days, I will not quit on this."

Integrity (Your Inner Contract)

Please reflect and write down your answers.

What integrity means to me:

____

____

Areas where I must be more honest with myself:

____

____

Nonnegotiable values I will not compromise:

____

____

How integrity protects my long-term future:

____

____

Personal oath: "I choose self-respect over shortcuts."

Consistency (the Silent Superpower)

Please track and write down your answers.

One habit I must practice consistently:

____

____

Small actions I can do daily:

____

____

What usually breaks my consistency:

____

____

My life and my promise:

____

____

Daily truth: "Small actions done daily create massive change."

ACKNOWLEDGMENTS

I come from humble roots, and the people around me have shaped every step of my journey. I want to acknowledge my brothers, sisters, close friends, relatives, and colleagues—those who supported me and even those who doubted me. Each one played a part in teaching me valuable lessons that helped me move forward with greater strength and clarity.

A special acknowledgment goes to **Sonal,** my true companion, whose presence has been my anchor and inspiration. And to **Kiaan & Kiarav**, my lifeline, whose love and energy give meaning to everything I do.

Thank you all for being a part of my story.

ABOUT THE AUTHOR

Brijendra Dharampuria, also known simply as Bri, is an entrepreneur, a leader, a survivor, and a first-generation achiever whose life journey spans two countries and countless lessons. Growing up with humble beginnings, he carried an inner promise to create a life far beyond the limitations he was born into—a promise that fueled his determination and shaped his destiny.

A survivor of a tragic, near-fatal accident, Bri's perspective on life deepened in ways that only true adversity can teach. The phases of marriage, fatherhood, leadership, and rebuilding after life-changing challenges gave him a rare clarity about resilience, purpose, and the strength hidden within every human being.

As an entrepreneur, Bri built businesses from scratch, led diverse teams, and created opportunities that influenced many lives. His leadership is driven by courage, compassion, and a commitment to continuous growth. Every mistake he made became a lesson, every setback became a stepping stone, and every achievement became a reminder of what consistent effort and integrity can build.

Through *The MAGIC of Life*, Bri shares the philosophy that shaped his journey—embracing mistakes, developing the right approach, setting meaningful goals, living with integrity, and practicing daily consistency. His intention is to inspire readers to rise above limitations, find direction in their own struggles, and discover the magic already inside them.

Today Bri lives in the United States with his family, continuing to build, lead, and inspire through his work, his experiences, and his unwavering belief in the power of transformation.

Thank you for walking through the MAGIC of Life.

If this book inspired you, helped you grow, or touched your journey in any way, I would love to stay connected.

Follow my work, thoughts, and future projects at www. brimagic.com.

"If this book stays with you,
let it be because it reminds you
who you are becoming."